Jack McArdle SS CC

I Believe in the Resurrection of the Body

Thoughts from the Catechism of the Catholic Church on Death, Judgment, Hell, Heaven and Purgatory

VERITAS

First published 1995 by
Veritas Publications
7-8 Lower Abbey Street
Dublin 1

ISBN 1 85390 289 6

The numbers in parenthesis throughout the text refer to the paragraphs of the *Catechism of the Catholic Church*,

Cover design by Bill Bolger
Printed in Ireland by Paceprint Ltd, Dublin

Introduction

My theme here is what used be called 'the Four Last Things', Death, Judgment, Hell and Heaven, with more than just a passing reference to Purgatory. As I read what the Catechism has to say about each of these areas, I was struck by one thing in particular. With all our progress in so many fields, including, it must be said, the field of theology, the teaching contained in this section is basically what my parents learned in their Penny Catechism. There is something about death that survives (if I may use the word!) all attempts of medicine, psychoanalysis, or even theology, to belittle it, or to avoid the stark reality it presents.

Generally, there seems to be a certain ambivalence about death, where people are just not sure how to deal with it. Should I face up to it now, or wait till it approaches me? One thing is sure: we shall all die one day. Life, as we know it, is a journey from one birth to another birth. There is the womb life, the womb of life, and the fullness of life. The labour ward, where the baby enters the second stage of life, can be a foreshadowing of the terminally-ill ward, from which the person moves on to the third and final stage of life. Life, of course, never ends, so this final stage is eternal.

When I reach that third and final stage of life, I will then be all that God created me to be. In the meantime, there is a constant struggle between what I am, and what I ought to be; between what I want, and what I need; between what I ought to do, and what I'd like to do. This involves the struggle and tensions of life. As with the electrical socket in the wall, without a negative and a positive wire, there is no power. Without the struggle and the tension, there is no compassion, no empathy, no understanding of fellow-travellers on life's journey. On the other hand, if you ever wake up some morning, and find that your life is exactly the way it ought to be, please don't move; just stay there, and wait till the undertaker arrives!

Death in General

I said earlier that life is a journey from one birth to another. At the first birth, the cord is cut, and I leave that first stage behind. At my second birth, the pulling up of the straps from the coffin is a symbol of yet another cutting, another letting-go of a particular stage of life. Life, however, once it begins, never ends. If I draw a line along the wall, off to the horizon and off to infinity, and then I put two marks on that line, about two inches apart, it would help illustrate the fact that I spend an infinitesimal amount of my existence in the body.

The body is not me. I live in the body for a certain number of years, and then, because of wear, tear, or mishap, the body will no longer be habitable, and I will leave it, and go on to the next stage of life. I will never go into a coffin. I carry a donor card in my wallet, giving permission for any workable parts of the body to be made available to others after I've finished with them! The body is like the rockets on a space shuttle, which give propulsion and direction, and are then discarded, and fall back to earth. Imagine what it might look like under the ground in the middle of spring. There are dead bulbs and tubers everywhere, and I would completely fail to understand the reality if I were not aware of the whole new life that has appeared above the ground.

There were some grubs in the bottom of a pond. They were wondering whatever happens to those who climb the stems of the lilies to the top, and who never return. They agreed among themselves that the next one called to the surface should come back, and tell the others what life is like up there. Some time later, one of the grubs felt the urge to climb the stem of the lily. When he reached the top, his eyes opened in amazement. It was so bright and so warm up here, compared to the cold and dullness of below. Then an extraordinary thing began to happen. He began to unfold, as it were, and to open out, until eventually, he had developed into the most beautiful dragonfly you could ever imagine. (He had been created to become a dragonfly, but thought he was destined to remain a grub all his life.) Anyhow, as he flew back and forth across the pond, he could see his friends below, but they couldn't see him. Gradually, two things dawned on him. Firstly, there was no way he could manage to get back to them now; and, secondly, even if he did, they would never recognise such a beautiful creature as ever having been one of them.

We sometimes hear it said that 'no one comes back to tell us', and I'm glad they don't, because we just wouldn't understand a word they said. Imagine, if you can, an unborn baby with perfect hearing. Now try speaking to the baby. Is there one single word in any language that the baby would understand? Water, rain, toy, food ...not one word would mean a thing to the baby. There is a similar gap between this present stage and the next, and scripture tells us that 'no eye has seen, nor ear heard, nor the human heart conceived, what God has prepared for those who love him' (*I Cor 2:9*).

A man and his four-year-old son were strolling through a cemetery on a Sunday afternoon. The young lad pointed to the graves and asked: 'Daddy, what are those?' The father was taken aback, not sure how to explain such a thing as death to someone so young. Anyhow, he had a go, and he told him that graves were for people who had lived in those houses down there, and then, one day, Holy God sent for them to come to live in his house with all his angels. The young lad thought about this for a while, and then he asked: 'And Daddy, did they go off to live in Holy God's house with all his angels?' 'Yes, they did', replied the father, hoping he would not be pressed for any further details. The young lad thought for another few seconds, and then his face lit up with understanding as he remarked: 'And do you know what,

Daddy, I bet when they went off to live in Holy God's house, this is where they left their clothes.'

Belief in Resurrection

Quite apart from any religious teachings or beliefs, there is a basic instinct for survival, a sort of primitive resilience within the human spirit that betokens ongoing life. On the darkest day, there is always the hope that tomorrow will be better. All human endeavours, all inventions, all discoveries have come about out of a desire to make tomorrow a little bit better. Without fully understanding it, the most primitive tribes believed in an after-life, some sort of spirit world, where life would continue in some other form. The Christian teaching about resurrection brings this very definitely and clearly to a much higher plateau.

> Belief in the resurrection of the dead has been an essential element of the Christian faith from the beginning. 'The confidence of Christians is the resurrection of the dead; believing this we live'. (*Tertullian*)
>
> 'If the Spirit of him who raised Jesus from the dead dwells in you, he who raised Christ Jesus from the dead will give life to your mortal bodies also, through his Spirit who dwells in you.' (*Rom 8:11*) (*989*)

Right from the beginning, the Catechism bases all our hope of resurrection on the fact of the Resurrection of Jesus.

> How can some of you say there is no resurrection of the dead? But if there is no resurrection of the dead, then Christ has not been raised; if Christ has not been raised, then our preaching is in vain.... But in fact Christ has been raised from the dead, the first fruits of those who have fallen asleep. (*I Cor 15:12-14. 20*) (*991*)

God was looked upon as creator of the whole person, body and soul. He was seen as a God who was faithful to his promises, and who stood by what he created. His creation was ongoing, evolving, opening out to greater things. He was not a God who created just to destroy again. God does not change, but is 'the same yesterday, today, and always' (*Heb 13:8*). When we messed up his plans for us, he continued to create, to bring order out of chaos. I would suggest that the ability of a person to hope in the face of all odds is a reflection of that part of us that is made in God's image and likeness. We see this faith in resurrection expressed very early in the Bible with the account of the Maccabean martyrs going to their death:

> The King of the universe will raise us up to an everlasting renewal of life, because we have died for his laws. One cannot but choose to die at the hands of men, and to cherish the hope that God gives of being raised again by him. (*II Macc 7:14*) (*992*)
>
> Faith in the resurrection rests on faith in God, who 'is not a God of the dead, but of the living'. (*Mk12:27*) (*993*)

Christ's Resurrection and Ours

Jesus links faith in the resurrection to his own person.

> 'I am the Resurrection and the life'. (*Jn 11:25*) It is Jesus himself who on the last day will raise up those who have believed in him, who have eaten his body, and drunk his blood. (*Jn 6:40*) (*994*)

On several occasions during his life on earth, Jesus showed that he had power over death. One of his stories tells us about the good wheat that the farmer sowed in his field. And then the weeds appeared, because of original sin. 'An enemy has done this', said the farmer. The servants asked if they might pull up the weeds, and the farmer said no, that he would take care of that himself, because, in pulling up the weeds, they might damage the wheat as well (*Mt 13:24-30*). The weeds that were sown in the wheat of our creation were sin, sickness and death. Jesus came to remove those weeds. He forgave sin, healed sickness, and proved, through his death and Resurrection, that he had overcome death.

During his life, Jesus was challenged about his claim to forgive sin. 'Who can forgive sins but God?' (*Mk 2:7*). To prove that 'the Son of Man has authority on earth to forgive sin', he told the paralysed man to get up and walk (*Mk 2:8-9*). In other words, he has equal power over sickness and sin, and he would prove again and again that he was in full control of both. His power to drive out demons further witnessed to his authority over evil of every kind. And then, 'the last enemy to be destroyed was death' (*I Cor 15:26*).

When Jesus headed towards Jerusalem, he knew that he was facing the final show-down with death. This was a total act of trust in the Father's love and promises, and it was putting into practice all he had said before about trusting in the Father's love. He yielded up his spirit to the Father in the belief that the Father would return that spirit to him. This was to bring the sacrifice of Abraham one step further (*Gen 22:1-19*). Abraham was asked to sacrifice his son Isaac, and, when he showed that he was willing to obey, God accepted his good will, and Isaac was spared.

On Calvary, God went one step further in that he, the Father, did actually permit the death of his Son, and then, after the sacrifice was made, he brought his Son safely through death, and into a life that was eternal, and forever free of the trammels of death. In that act, death had been deprived of victory, and had been overcome. 'Where, O death, is your victory? Where, O death, is your sting?' (*I Cor 15:55-56*). For all time, then, the presence of God among us, in the Incarnation of Jesus, will be seen in terms of his victory over the three evils of sin, sickness and death.

> To be a witness to Christ is to be a 'witness to his Resurrection', to '[have eaten and drunk] with him after he rose from the dead' (*Acts 1:22; 10:41*). Encounters with the risen Christ characterise the Christian hope of resurrection. We shall rise like Christ, with him, and through him (*995*).

Witnessing to the Resurrection of Christ is central to the vocation of a Christian. Again and again after his Resurrection, Jesus appeared to his disciples. He ate with them, he invited them to touch him, he did everything within his power to prove to them that he was really alive, and not just a ghost. This was very important, because they were to be witnesses throughout the world to his Resurrection. Christians must bring resurrection to the world in which they live. The only real sin for a Christian is to lose hope, because it means living without the eternal hope that must be part of the spirit of a risen people.

Peter and Judas were guilty of a betrayal that was very similar, because each put himself or his greed before Jesus. What followed, however, was totally different in each case. Judas thought he had put himself outside of Jesus' love, he despaired, and hanged himself. That was his ultimate rejection of God. Peter, on the other hand, still clung to his belief in Jesus' love for him, and when Jesus turned and looked at Peter, Peter went outside and wept bitterly (*Lk 22:61-62*). Peter knew that Jesus still loved him, that nothing had changed. Jesus loved because Jesus was good, and not because Peter was deserving of that love. No surprise, then, that Peter would later write these words: 'Always have a reason to give to those who ask you the reason for the hope that you have' (*I Pt 3:15*).

It is the Christian belief that we have died with Christ, and we have risen with Christ, and the victory is already ours, should we choose to accept it. 'Lord, by your cross and resurrection, you have set us free; you are the Saviour of the world'. Death was 'the final enemy', and Jesus overcame that, so there is no reason for despair.

> From the beginning, Christian faith in the resurrection has met with incomprehension and opposition. 'On no point does the Christian faith encounter more opposition than on the resurrection of the body'. (*St Augustine*) (*996*)
>
> When Peter and John were talking to the people, the priests came up to them, accompanied by the captain of the Temple and the Sadducees. They were extremely annoyed that they were teaching the people the doctrine of the resurrection from the dead, by proclaiming the resurrection of Jesus. (*Acts 4:1-2*)

The Catechism asks, and answers, some very central questions on resurrection. For example, 'What is rising?' 'Who will rise?' 'How?' 'When?' The answers can be summarised as follows. Rising is what happens when God grants incorruptible life to the body, which, from a human perspective, has long since decayed; when he reunites the body with the soul, something that is made possible because of the victory of Jesus. Jesus went to great lengths after his Resurrection to prove beyond all doubt that he really had overcome death. Unlike Lazarus, who was brought back to life, and who, once again, would have to die, Jesus had passed through death, and had come out the other side into total freedom, still in possession of the body he had before death. The disciples had to be convinced that, yes, this was Jesus, not a ghost. He invited them to touch him, to give him something to eat, to prove to themselves that he was really bodily present to them. Once again, he came to them, walking on the waters; he repeated the miracle of the large catch of fish, and he even prepared breakfast for them, joining them in the meal (*Jn 21:1-14*).

> All the dead will rise, 'those who have done good, to the resurrection of life, and those who have done evil, to the resurrection of judgement'. (*Jn 5:29*) (*998*)

How this will happen is something we accept on faith, because it is not possible for us to understand something that is outside of our experience. When I eat food, it is changed into what I am. The blood that flows through my veins has come from food that I ate. When I receive the Lord Jesus in Eucharist, the opposite happens; I am changed more and more into him. 'Those who eat my flesh, and drink my blood have eternal life, and I will raise them up on the last day.' (*Jn 6:54*).

And, finally, to the question When? the Catechism tells us that all this will happen when Jesus comes again (*1001*). When we examine some of the longer post-Pentecost sermons of the Apostles, we see that they are divided into four sections, each given equal importance: The Messiah you have longed for has come, and his name is Jesus. You killed him, but he rose again from the dead. He returned to the Father, and he sent the Holy Spirit to complete his work on earth. Lastly, he will return again at the end of time, to proclaim eternal victory for his kingdom, and the end of the kingdoms of the world, and of Satan. The Second Coming of Jesus is included among what was seen as Good News. In the Mass we announce that, as Christians, 'we wait in joyful hope for the coming of our Saviour Jesus Christ'.

This final coming is often referred to as Christ's *Parousia*. There is a science called eschatology connected with this Second Coming. It speaks of something that is here now, but will not be totally here till the end of time. In other words, we already share in the resurrected life of Jesus, even if we must wait for a future time when we can fully experience the fullness of that sharing. I remember a young lad in my class in school who had been left a considerable amount of money, but he would not have access to all of it until he was twenty-one. When I knew him, his school fees and all his basic requirements were being met from that money, so in no way could he be considered poor, or deserving of our sympathy. He lived with the sure and certain hope that security was his in the foreseeable future. This thought must have helped through many a moment when he didn't have the cash he would have liked to have had. His hope was in the future, but it certainly helped him in the now.

> United with Christ by Baptism, believers already truly participate in the heavenly life of the risen Christ.... Nourished with his body in the Eucharist, we already belong to the Body of Christ. When we rise on the last day, we 'also will appear with him in glory'. (*Col 3:4*) (*1003*)

Dying in Jesus Christ

To rise with Christ, we must die with Christ. We must be willing to pass through the death of the Red Sea and the desert before we can expect to enter the Promised Land. Most of us have heard the phrase 'everybody wants to go to heaven, but nobody wants to die!' Death was not part of God's original plan for us, and, therefore, it is not something that is deeply embedded in our nature. For example, in the words of St Augustine, God made us for himself, and our hearts can never be at peace until they rest in him. Death, however, was not part of God's creation, and, therefore, even now, is a weed in the wheat of our souls. Death, like sin, is an invader, and does not naturally belong in our natures. That is why death could never be something that would have an instinctive appeal to an unredeemed human being.

Death is a direct result of sin, and it brings our earthly lives to an end. There is no 'reincarnation' after death. Death was a direct result of the original disobedience, and could only be redeemed through the total obedience of Jesus, an obedience which brought him all the way to death, 'even to death on a cross' (*Phil 2:8*). Through his obedience unto death, Jesus has turned what was a curse into a blessing (*1009*). Because of Christ, a Christian can now look on death as something very positive and profoundly meaningful. What was seen, literally, as a mortal enemy, has now been included as a necessary part of our journey to the fullness of life. It is a moment when God calls us home, and when Jesus can 'show us off', as it were, before the Father, because we, redeemed sinners, are the first fruits of his suffering, death and Resurrection.

> Every action of yours, every thought, should be those of one who expects to die before the day is out. Death would have no great terrors for you if you had a quiet conscience.... Then why not keep clear of sin, instead of running away from death? If you aren't fit to face death today, it's very unlikely you will be tomorrow... (*The Imitation of Christ 1, 23, 1*) (*1014*)

The Particular Judgment

At the moment of death, we come face to face with Christ, and we are faced with the consequences of accepting or rejecting him. Some theologians would say that there is one last opportunity to say yes or no at that very moment. This would answer the problem presented by those who have never heard of Christ, and who cannot, therefore, be punished for something over which they had no control. For someone to say yes at this late stage would be compatible with the story of the owner of the vineyard, who gave full wages to all the workers, irrespective of whether they had worked all day, or had joined the work-force at the last hour (*Mt 20:1-16*).

Our eternal destiny hinges on whether we accept or reject Jesus Christ. Nobody comes to the Father any other way (*Jn 14:6*). It matters not how or when that acceptance is expressed. Like the workers in the vineyard, full wages are offered to all who answer the call. This is pure gift, and cannot be earned. The danger of religion is that it can imply some element of 'meriting', as if we ourselves can merit redemption and salvation.

When I think of the many whose lives are snuffed out like a candle in a storm, I live with the hope and the expectation that, at the moment of being free of the body, and having the capacity for a clear and unclouded decision, they are given one last chance, as it were, to decide for or against Christ. I believe this because I do not accept that God can or does show favouritism. Some people have every possible opportunity to prepare for death, and are completely aware of its approach, while others are blown away in a tragedy, before they know what hit them. When one deals with tragedy in a family, it is not unusual to hear a parent or relative ask 'I wonder was he ready?' My only answer to that is to speak of a God of great love, who is more concerned about our salvation and well-being than we ourselves could ever be. Scripture tells us that God does not will the death of a sinner, but, rather, that he be converted and live.

There is nothing automatic about God! Nothing 'just happens', and coincidences and accidents can be God's way of preserving his anonymity! The essential factor in salvation is whether or not we say yes to it. St Paul says that we are saved by 'his blood and our faith' (*Rom 3:25*). Faith is a response to love, and I would strongly contend that a person who has lived in such circumstances in life that it would be unreasonable to expect him even to know that there is a God, let alone that God loves him, then we must accept the fact that God can mediate his salvation in some other way.

The idea that this might be immediately after the exact moment of death, when I see everything in the whole new unimpeded light of the spirit world; when I can see for myself in a flash, and will have the freedom to make a decision that is not circumscribed by human or worldly limitations, is a concept that speaks to me of a God of love and of justice, who does all he can to prevent the loss of a single soul.

I firmly believe that some people could say 'no' to God, even at that last moment, and I can understand how this might come about. For example, I believe that if Satan were offered forgiveness now, he would refuse it, because to accept it would imply an admission that he was wrong in the first place; his pride would not allow that. It follows, therefore, that human beings can be so strongly influenced, and in such bondage to the evil one that, at that last moment, they will reject every offer that God could make them, and will be eternally lost.

> The parable of the poor man Lazarus and the words of Christ on the cross to the good thief, as well as other New Testament texts, speak of a final destiny of the soul – a destiny which can be different for some and for others. (*1021*)

Heaven

At the Last Supper, Jesus tells the Father that he had not lost any of those whom the Father had entrusted to him.

> While I was with them, I protected them in your name… and not one of them was lost, except the one destined to be lost…. (*Jn 17:12*)

To remain within the fold of Jesus, the Good Shepherd, is to live in his kingdom. In eternity, that kingdom is called heaven. The kingdom is now. The shepherd knows his sheep, and they know him, they hear his voice, and they obey him. Heaven is everlasting kingdom, and the 'made-in-God's-image' part of us becomes totally evident and completed. At that stage, we will have become what God created us to be. We will have reached a place of perfect living, when everything about us will be totally compatible with the perfect life of the Trinity.

God's love is best expressed in his willingness to

forgive. Loving another implies a willingness to be open to ongoing forgiveness for that person's shortcomings and faults. If a couple kneel in front of me at a wedding service, I may know that they do not have a great deal of intelligence, or that they don't have much money, but if I can believe that they have enough forgiveness in their hearts for each other, then I will have hope that their love will survive. Forgiveness is the preservative that keeps love from 'going off'.

In heaven, I will be a sinner, but a sinner whom God forgave. In fact, it's probably a great bonus on the way to heaven to be convinced that I am a sinner. If I am willing to join the publican in his humble prayer of truth: 'O God, be merciful to me, a sinner' (*Lk 18:13*), then I, too, will be justified. To be justified is Scripture's way of saying that all sins are forgiven, all debts are wiped out, the process of total rehabilitation is complete. Heaven is where those who are justified live in complete and eternal union with God.

> Heaven is the ultimate end and fulfilment of the deepest human longings, the state of supreme, definitive happiness. (*1024*)

When Jesus went down into the Jordan in his baptism, we are told that 'the heaven was opened' (*Lk 3:21*). When Jesus bowed his head in death 'the curtain of the Temple was torn in two' (*Mk 15:38*), and, for the first time in history, access to the Holy of Holies was available. Heaven was open to those who belong to Christ, who accept and possess the fruits of the redemption, accomplished by his overcoming the Fall. Because of their openness to him, they will be filled with the fullness of his grace, and, like Mary, they, too, will be 'full of grace'.

> This mystery of blessed communion with God and all who are in Christ is beyond all understanding and description. Scripture speaks of it in images: life, light, peace, wedding feast, wine of the kingdom, the Father's house, the heavenly Jerusalem, paradise; 'no eye has seen, nor ear heard, nor the heart of man conceived, what God has prepared for those who love him'. (*I Cor 2:9*) (*1027*)

Purgatory

Life in heaven is a life of the blessed, a life which is completely redeemed and purified by the blood of the Lamb. This follows a total 'yes' to Christ, and to his gift of eternal salvation. A total 'no' will result in eternal alienation from God. Short of that total 'yes', however, are levels of less than perfect openness to the gift of salvation, which can leave one in a state of less than perfect purification, while still not meriting eternal condemnation. It is the teaching of the Church, since the early Council of Florence, the Council of Trent, and now in this new Catechism, that such souls undergo purification after death in order to achieve the holiness necessary to enter the joy of heaven.

Purgatory is not alienation from God. Its pain could

be in being deeply conscious of God, but not yet in a position to enjoy that 'beatific vision'. Purgatory is a time of waiting, of patient, patient waiting. It could also be a time for a great deal of reflection, bringing one gradually to the point of accepting the unconditional love of God.

It is often said that the saint is not the person who loves God, but rather the person who is totally convinced of God's love. My openness to God's love must surely be a major factor in the process of salvation. God's love is unconditional, but I can put my own conditions on it. To that extent I can greatly limit my capacity to accept and receive that love. God does not give me anything, he offers me everything, and it is totally up to me whether I accept it or not. Purgatory could well be a time of purification from such pride and stubbornness, where we are given time to reflect on the blocks put in the way of God's prodigal and generous love.

It has often been suggested that the souls in Purgatory can do very little to help themselves, and that they depend to a great extent on the prayers of others, within the communion of saints. This would seem ironic if their failure to enter heaven at the point of death was caused by a pride which prevented them accepting the total free gift of salvation, and led them to insisting on earning it themselves! It is also traditionally accepted that, while the souls in Purgatory may not be able to do much to help themselves, or improve their own condition, they can be a powerful source of good for those of us who pray for them. This is part of the belief in the Communion of Saints, where those in heaven can help us, while we can help those in Purgatory, and they, in turn, can obtain many blessings for us. It makes sense that, if they can obtain graces for us, the very fact of their exercising that love is essentially a purifying factor for them.

The practice of prayer for the dead has always been a tradition in the Church, and, indeed, long before the time of Jesus. In early Bible times Judas Maccabeus 'made atonement for the dead, so that they might be delivered from their sin' (*II Macc 12:45*). The Church has always given a special place to prayers for the dead, in the belief that such prayers help the souls during their time of purification.

> Let us help and commemorate them. If Job's sons were purified by their father's sacrifice, why should we doubt that our offerings for the dead bring them some consolation? Let us not hesitate to help those who have died, and to offer our prayers for them. (*St John Chrysostom*) (*1032*)

Hell

> He who does not love remains in death. Anyone who hates his brother is a murderer, and you know that no murderer has eternal life abiding in him. (*I Jn 3:14-15*) (*1033*)

As I've said before, God does not give me anything;

he offers me everything. Accepting or rejecting is my choice, my decision. God will not send me anywhere when I die. Rather will he eternalise the decisions I make in life. I cannot be united with God unless I freely choose to be. Jesus said that he never did or said anything unless the Father told him. He brought this one step further when he said 'If you keep my commandments, you will abide in my love, just as I have kept my Father's commandments and abide in his love' (*Jn 15:10*).

The flock is made up of both sheep and goats. Sheep follow the shepherd in total loyalty, while the goats just go along with wherever the action is. Jesus warns us that there will come a time when the sheep will be separated from the goats. There is nothing automatic about God! Everything is a deliberate and purposeful decision.

> To die in mortal sin, *in a state of unrepented alienation from God* [author's words], without repenting and accepting God's merciful love, means remaining separated from him for ever by our own free choice. This state of definitive self-exclusion from communion with God, and the blessed, is called 'hell'. (*1033*)

The real me, that inner-self me, is made in God's image, and I can never find happiness or fulfilment apart from God. There is an emptiness in the human heart that can never be filled by anything less than God. Belonging to God is a basic intrinsic human need. Being separated from God for all eternity is the worst possible human agony.

> God predestines no one to hell; for this, a wilful turning away from God (a mortal sin) is necessary, and persistence in it until the end. In the Eucharistic liturgy, and in the daily prayers of her faithful, the Church implores the mercy of God, who does not want 'any to perish, but all to come to repentance'. (*II Pt 3:9*) (*1037*)

There is something chilling and 'deadly' about the whole idea of hell. When we remember that it is love, unconditional love for us, that is being rejected, then there appears to be some kind of fatalistic insanity at play. Human nature is extraordinarily complex, and can cause any one of us to reject the very thing that we need and want most of all. To live with hatred is to live in the darkest dungeon. Such a person is in a prison of his or her own making. To live in this way for eternity is beyond all human comprehension. I think of God as ready to bend over backwards to prevent this, because, once the decision is made, there is no going back, the die is cast forever. We sometimes hear it said that 'God is a God of love, and how could he possibly send someone to hell for all eternity?' What is chilling about hell, for me, is that God does not send anyone there, and he is deeply disappointed that anyone should so reject his love that they should opt for an eternity in hell, rather than have him love, redeem and save them.

Limbo

There is no reference at all in the Catechism to Limbo. The very word 'Limbo' came to mean neither here nor there. It was originally thought of as something positive, as something that was seen as being part of the economy of salvation, without the benefit of Baptism; certainly not at all in the same category as Hell. Unfortunately, with time, this came to be thought of as something negative, as something that implied a permanent separation from God. Thankfully, this is no longer accepted as part of the plan of a loving God.

> '...the great mercy of God who desires that all men should be saved, and Jesus' tenderness toward children which caused him to say: "Let the children come to me, do not hinder them", allow us to hope that there is a way of salvation for children who have died without Baptism.' (*1261*)

The Last Judgment

> Do not be surprised at this: the hour is coming when all those living in tombs will hear my voice and come out; those who have done good shall rise to live, and those who have done evil shall rise to be condemned. (*Jn 5:28-29*)

How often do we hear that justice must be done, and that justice must be seen to be done? God is a God of love, and he is also a God of justice. Might I suggest that, in creation, he was a God of love. In

Jesus Christ, he became a God of mercy. And, finally, he becomes a God of justice, where all that is good and bad becomes revealed. When God created 'He saw that it was good' (*Gen 1:10*). When Adam and Eve 'fell' for the lie in the Garden, they came under new 'management'; they came under the influence of the 'Father of lies' (*Jn 8:44*). Salvation is all about rescuing us from the kingdom of Satan (lies, deceit etc.), and bringing us into the kingdom of God, where we 'learn to live and to walk in the Spirit', and are brought into all truth, and the truth sets us free (*Jn 16:13; 8:32*). The triumph of Christ over Satan is made final and positive when everything is exposed to the light, and no lie will remain hidden. In the presence of Christ, who is Truth itself, everything will be laid bare – the good, the bad, the ugly.

> The Last Judgment will come when Christ returns in glory. Only the Father knows the day and the hour; only he determines the moment of its coming. Then through his Son Jesus Christ he will pronounce the final word on all history. We shall know the ultimate meaning of the whole work of creation and of the entire economy of salvation, and understand the marvellous ways by which his Providence led everything towards its final end. The Last Judgment will reveal that God's justice triumphs over all the injustices committed by his creatures, and that God's love is stronger than death. (*1040*)

I have quoted at some length from the Catechism on the subject of the General Judgment, because I believe the previous paragraph to be a powerful statement that requires reflection. In the final analysis, God is the beginning and the end, he always was, and ever shall be. It is right and fitting that God should have the final word on all history.

It could well be a source of surprise, if not 'religious' scandal, to learn that the General Judgment will deal with things that will be rather materialistic, like a coat, a slice of bread, or a cup of water. As we read the words of Jesus (*Mt 25*), we might be surprised to learn that there are no questions about prayers, religious experiences, or Church celebrations. Rather will we be asked about love in all its forms, for all of God's children. We will discover that Christ has identified himself very closely with the poor, the outcast, the marginalised. 'Just as you did this to one of the least of these who are members of my family, you did it to me' (*Mt 25:40*).

I taught in schools for many years, and I know just how important exam questions can be in the life of the student, both in the short-term and the long-term. Imagine if I could give the class a copy of the questions they will get in their final exam four years from now! I would have friends for life, and pity the poor teacher trying to interest them in an area of the syllabus that will not figure in that final exam! If, when all is over, a student has still done badly, then, at least, there can be no excuses. Let me take that idea one step further, when I see Matthew 25 providing the questions which will face each of us in the most important and crucial examination of all time. Is it reasonable to expect that we should be prepared? In this I think that God is more than generous, more than just.

A New Heaven and a New Earth

The Bible brings us from the original plan of God, through the Fall, on to Redemption, and it leaves us with the hope of eternal victory. In this victory, God's original plan is redeemed, people once again walk with God in friendship, as in the Garden. In other words, the God who created has now re-created, and has made all things new again. Sacred Scripture calls this renewal 'a new heaven and a new earth', where all things in heaven and on earth will be united under Christ.

> For man, this consummation will be the final realisation of the unity of the human race, which God willed from creation.... Those who are united in Christ will form the community of the redeemed.... The beatific vision, in which God opens himself in an inexhaustible way to the elect, will be the ever-flowing well-spring of happiness, peace, and mutual communion. (1045)

For the cosmos, Revelation affirms that, just as people will be transformed, so too will the material universe. It will be restored to its original state, to be at the service of the just, sharing with them their glorification in the risen Jesus Christ. (1046)

> For the creation waits with eager longing for the revealing of the sons of God... in hope because the creation itself will be set free from its bondage to decay.... We know that the whole creation has been groaning in travail together until now; and not only the creation, but we ourselves, who have the first fruits of the Spirit, groan inwardly as we wait for adoption as sons, the redemption of our bodies (Rm 8:19-23).

In effect, this will mean a return to the Garden, where nothing else will exist that can ever again spoil God's plan of love for his children. The kingdom of Satan, with its lies and deceits, and the kingdom of this world, with its wrong priorities and false gods, will have come to an end, and there will only be the Kingdom where Jesus Christ will be Lord. All the enemies will be put under his feet (*I Cor 15:25*).

> In this new universe, the heavenly Jerusalem, God will have his dwelling among men (*Rev 21:5*). 'He will wipe away every tear from their eyes, and death shall be no more, neither shall there be mourning nor crying nor pain any more, for the former things have passed away'. (*Rev 21:4*) (*1044*)

In this final and eternal transformation all will be changed, changed utterly. God will be in all, and all of his creation will be in perfect harmony. The heavens, the earth, the cosmos, will all show forth the glory of God, and people will rejoice in their heavenly home-coming, after the struggles of their years in exile.

Conclusion

What impressed me most, as I studied this section of the Catechism, was the sheer richness of it. No words of mine could do justice to the wealth of references, quotations, and resource material that it contains. This is a veritable gold-mine for anyone with a reflective spirit, who wishes to nourish the soul with solid teaching, and benefit from thousands of years of prayer and reflection. This richness is greatly enhanced by the priority given to Scripture references in support of particular teachings.

I am not suggesting that the Catechism would make ideal 'bedtime reading', but, for the Catholic who is interested in being informed, and being formed with authentic Church teaching, then I would strongly recommend it.

From earliest years, I had thought of the 'Four Last Things' as off-putting and frightening. I found the Catechism dealing with them with gentleness, and with an approach that was far from dogmatic. I found myself called constantly to reflect on my own particular input, and to see how my own personal choices could greatly influence the outcome of events. This was inspiring, because I felt that, rather than state everything in black and white, the Catechism was inviting me to get involved, in the certain knowledge that I did actually have a very major part to play in my own eternal destiny.

I am truly grateful to have had the opportunity to reflect on this section of the Catechism, and to share some of those reflections with others. I pray that you, the reader, may also be blessed, and that these short reflections may be the door through which you might enter, to savour some of the many other 'refreshments' contained in the Catechism of the Catholic Church.